# Preaching a Sermon Series with Common Worship

### Phillip Tovey

Training Officer Diocese of Oxford

## GROVE BOOKS LIMITED
RIDLEY HALL RD· CAMBRIDGE  CB3 9HU

# Contents

### Acknowledgements

I want to thank Revd Roger James, Revd Bruce Gillingham, Revd Mark Earey, Ven Trevor Lloyd, and Revd Helen Kendrick for their encouragement and comments on early drafts of this book.

**The Cover Illustration** is by Peter Ashton

**First Impression** February 2004
**ISSN** 0144-1728
**ISBN** 1 85174 554 8

# Introduction

1

## *Why do many churches not preach sermon series?*

While the lectionary has now provided sequential reading from week to week, in many places the sermon seems to hop around from one lesson to another, epistle one week, gospel the next, not showing any connection with the week before. There may be good reasons for this:

- There is no tradition of the sermon series in this congregation.
- People only come irregularly and so this is not worth doing.
- It is a restriction on a preacher to keep to a series.
- It is too difficult to get the preachers coordinated.
- A series is seen as only an activity for middle class churches or student churches

These may seem like good reasons but there is an honoured tradition of sequential preaching through scripture and one that we should not neglect lightly.

In the history of preaching there have been periods when preaching though the Bible was common. This we will look at in the next chapter. There are good reasons why we should consider continuing the practice, which include:

- The need for people to understand the Bible better.
- The possibility of giving some systematic teaching.
- Helping people to get an understanding of the different books of the Bible.
- Showing the different genres of the Bible.
- Learning from the experience of the biblical stories.

While some churches have specialized in this type of preaching, it is possible that all of us could do this from time to time. I found that sermon series were popular in an ordinary country church which had no tradition of preaching series.

The recent liturgical changes in the church might be a point to reconsider the possibility of a series on a biblical book. Many churches now use the Revised Common Lectionary or a lectionary based on it. It is constructed on the theory of sequential reading from week to week. The preacher who gets up and says 'I don't see how these readings connect today' has misunderstood the way the lectionary works. One synoptic gospel is read through each year. Epistles get read in sequence. In one track there is continuous reading of the Old Testament as compared to an Old Testament lesson thematically related to the Gospel. For a large part of the year the readings are sequential from week to week. It is an easy step to turn this into a series as we shall see.

*The recent liturgical changes in the church might be a point to reconsider a series on a biblical book*

The *Service of the Word* allows an open season in the lectionary and this is explained in the *New Patterns for Worship*. This gives even greater freedom. In one way this is encouraging us to consider the possibility of a series, and in another it has provided off-the-peg examples. We shall also look at this provision later.

My interest in a sermon series came out of further study on preaching. There are many fine books on preaching but most lead up to preaching an individual sermon. There seems to be a gap in the literature on putting together a series, the issues in doing that, and the overall strategy for preaching throughout the years. This booklet is a beginning to look at these issues.

So why do we not do sermon series? One big objection is of people's patterns of attendance. Paddy Benson and John Roberts showed in a recent survey that there are many people who are regulars but not every week.[1] This means that each sermon must stand alone but that does not mean that we cannot preach a series. There are weekly attenders and my experience has been that people have realized that a series is

*Such enquiry is fostered by the sense of momentum built by a series*

going on and ask questions of what happened in between. Such enquiry is fostered by the sense of momentum built by a series. It might be that we need to make provision for those who have missed a week, for example by making notes available after the service.

Another objection comes from the caricature of expository preaching being of three points on the meaning of a word in a particular verse. While this approach may fit some of the epistles, a broader strategy will be required for the more narrative passages of the Bible. A series does not have to turn into such a tight version of exposition. Nor is preaching a sermon series the expression of one type of church tradition, as we will see in the next chapter. Indeed history shows that there have been a number of models of preaching a series.

Perhaps the question should be put the other way: Why *should* we do it? The answer is clear: to enable people to understand the Scriptures better in a more systematic way. A sequence of sermons each based on a passage or theme but without coherence from week to week may give inspiration and encouragement, but it will be hard for this to produce a more systematic knowledge. A sermon series can help plant an understanding of the books of the Bible and the great stories of redemption. There is a need for this to be supplemented by individual Bible reading and study groups, but the sermon can give this foundational knowledge to those who are regular but not usually involved in mid-week activities. There is still an important place for the sermon series in today's church.

# 2         Historical Examples of the Sermon Series

*There are good historical examples that suggest the use of the sermon series.*

Part of the aim of this book is to persuade people to consider the sermon series. This chapter will look at some key examples of the sermon series before looking at possibilities today. In the history of preaching there have been periods when preaching though the Bible was more common:

- The patristic period gives examples of this, for example the sermons of Chrysostom and Augustine.[2]

- The continental Reformation included the regular preaching on biblical books.

- The Puritans were also keen on this type of preaching. They moved on to more detailed exposition only looking at a few verses.[3]

- Sermon series were a part of the Evangelical Revival, for example Charles Simeon and JC Ryle.

- Recent evangelical preaching has emphasized sermon series, for example Martin Lloyd Jones and his sermons on Romans or John Stott and the preaching at All Souls Langham Place.

This is not to say that everyone must do sequential preaching all the time but there are good examples for history that might encourage us not to neglect the idea.

## Patristic Examples

Chrysostom and Augustine provide about half of the material on patristic preaching.[4] They both regularly preached, sometimes daily through biblical books. Not all of their material survived, but some of their material is now readily available in English, not least on a CD ROM. This puts their work easily into our hands.

The surviving material on Augustine includes these sermons:

| | |
|---|---|
| Gospel lessons | 97 |
| Homilies on John | 107 |
| 1 John | 10 |
| Psalms | Sermons on every psalm |

On the Gospel of John we see Augustine preaching sequentially (also called *lectio continua*) sometimes taking passages but stopping at important points to preach on one verse. The introduction to the sermons on 1 John shows that a certain festival had interrupted his consecutive preaching and so he was going to do a short series on 1 John. This all sounds very much like today. So a very long series was broken up by something shorter, but he chose 1 John to do this because he thought it complemented his sermons on the Gospel. All of this was done in in or around 416.

Chrysostom has left a number of sermons, some of these dating back to his time in Antioch.

| | |
|---|---|
| Matthew | 90 |
| John | 88 |
| Acts | 55 |
| Romans | 32 |
| 1 Corinthians | 44 |
| 2 Corinthians | 30 |
| Galatians | 6 |
| Ephesians | 9 |
| Philippians | 15 |
| Colossians | 12 |
| 1 Thessalonians | 11 |
| 2 Thessalonians | 3 |
| Hebrews | 34 |

Again these are consecutive sermons working through these books of the Bible.

Most of these sermons were copied down by a stenographer while being preached. There was a tradition of daily preaching in certain periods, for example, Lent. However, our interest here is in their sermon series, which were consecutive, working through a book of the Bible in shorter or longer passages.

# Reformation Examples

Luther began to consider the place of preaching from 1523. He kept to the traditional Epistle and Gospel for Sunday morning but preached verse by verse at the weekday services. Thus the pattern in Wittenberg by 1526 became:

| | |
|---|---|
| Sunday morning | Traditional Epistle and Gospel |
| Sunday evening | Old Testament |
| Monday and Tuesday | Catechetical preaching |
| Wednesday | Matthew |
| Thursday and Friday | the Epistles |
| Saturday | John.[5] |

Luther began to preach on the Gospel of John in 1537. This he continued to do for a number of years. One of the characteristics of the continental Reformation is the way in which the university teachers of theology (like Luther) were also great preachers and that daily services included preaching.

Calvin likewise was an advocate of sequential preaching. He preached on the Gospel on Sundays and then a team of preachers led the weekday services. Calvin preached every other week. However, he was prevailed upon to preach more and at one time was preaching daily. He preached through books of the Old and New Testament and a large corpus of his sermons still survives. Perhaps 200 sermons on Deuteronomy might seem excessive, but to the people of his day this was fresh, as they had not heard such a steady diet of biblical teaching before.

## Puritans

The Puritans introduced great preaching to the English church. The Reformation in England occurred at first with a dearth of preachers. Having Bibles in church and reading Scripture was one of the drivers of reformation in England; 'the lectionary of the first prayer book of Edward VI opened up the whole of Scripture to the great mass of Englishmen in a way it had never been opened up before.'[6] It was the Puritans who were to bring a reform of preaching to England.

*It was the Puritans who were to bring a reform of preaching to England*

It is clear from William Perkins that he intended preaching to be expository. He summarizes that his book is intended to help preachers to read the text, explain the text in the light of other scriptures, and apply it, in straightforward plain speech.[7] This was developed by the Puritans into series both on topics and on biblical books. Thus Richard Sibbes preached a series on holiness *The Bruised Reed and the Smoking Flax* and other series on Philippians 2 and 3, Hosea 14, and 2 Corinthians 1 and 4. At this point there is no need to review the preaching strategies of the Puritans as this is well told elsewhere. What is important to point out is that they concentrated on sermon series that were either topical, or sequential on a book or chapter.

> The Puritans made a number of departures from the homiletic practice of the sixteenth century. They did not always follow the Reformers in using the form of the patristic homily, that is, a running commentary on a number of verses of Scripture. They did intend to do expository preaching... but they used much of the scholastic method as well.[8]

Thus the exposition came to be on a verse in a chapter rather than a number of verses. In the end the text was in danger of being a pretext when a thematic series was being produced. It is the worst excesses of this that began to give the sermon series a bad name.

## The Twentieth Century

This chapter is not attempting to give an exhaustive history of preaching or even of sermon series. However, there have been important examples of this in recent church life. Many will know the work of Martin Lloyd Jones at Westminster Chapel. Following the Puritan example Lloyd Jones preached through the Sermon on the Mount and more famously through Romans. This produced a number of volumes of sermons, sometimes looking at one verse a number of times.

Anglicans have not been averse to sermon series. William Temple, while at St James Piccadilly, preached through the Gospel of John in four years. This was to become a book, *Readings in St John's Gospel*.[9] John Stott advocates the sermon series in his classic *I Believe in Preaching*. He finds a number of reasons for Bible series:

- It forces us to look at passages we might otherwise avoid.
- It avoids curiosity as to why the preacher has chosen their text.
- It opens up people's horizons to the Scriptures.[10]

Stott wrote this while the ASB was in operation. The coming of *Common Worship* makes these aims even more achievable. Stott's practice was to preach on a passage of Scripture rather than individual verses as this allowed more Scripture to be covered over a number of years. These series then became the basis for a number of his books.[11]

## Conclusion

Thus there are many examples of preaching through the Scriptures in a systematic way in the history of preaching. This is not just confined to reformers, Puritans, and evangelicals, but was also the work of the fathers and others. The aim of the new lectionary resources for the church is for more Scripture to be read and much of it in sequence. This is an opportune time for some sequential preaching.

# Preaching a series from the Lectionary

3

*The present lectionary of the church just begs the preacher to use it for sermon series.*

When RCL came out I immediately used it to preach a number of sermon series. The continuous reading of the books of the Bible in ordinary time suggested to me that there were great possibilities for sequential preaching on biblical books. This may be because my formative years as a young Christian were in churches that did this anyway. However, I was perplexed by the response of colleagues and friends. Some lamented the death of a theme (I had got rather fed up with this in the ASB) and so either hunted for one that was not there or latched on to it when it was there. Others told me that liturgical preaching means that you have to preach on the Gospel. Again this perplexed me because what are the other books for? Of course one choice is to make the Old Testament lesson typologically linked to the Gospel reading. Following this track probably reinforces the idea of preaching on the Gospel. I had decided to go for the continuous reading seeing the possibility of nine years of sermons coming up.

## Some Principles of the Common Worship Lectionary

Lectionaries may not seem the most interesting part of our worship. However, they are crucial for the congregation to hear the Word of God and for the preacher to unfold its counsel. The Church of England's Principal Service provision is from the ecumenical Revised Common Lectionary based on the Roman Catholic Sunday Mass lectionary. This has some basic principles that are essential to grasp:

- The aim was to significantly increase the amount of Scripture read at the Communion. Thus three lessons, including one from the Old Testament and a psalm were provided for each Sunday over a three-year cycle. Each of the years concentrates on one synoptic gospel with John included in the rest of the year. This leads to considerably more Scripture being read than any other lectionary provided so far. This is to be welcomed as an improvement in the system.

- The period around the principal feasts of Christmas and Easter are provided with thematic readings to bring out these key events of salvation history. It is not just the festivals themselves but also the periods of preparation (Advent and Lent) that have these special readings.

- Ordinary time is provided with continuous or related reading of the lessons. One of the revisions to the Roman Catholic lectionary was to detach the Old Testament lesson from being typologically connected to the Gospel , the related approach. Thus there is the option of continuous Old Testament reading in ordinary time.

These key principles and the rules that surround them give expression to the preaching possibilities of the lectionary.

## Open and Closed Seasons in the Lectionary

The rules to govern lectionary use allow for variation from the lectionary at some times in the year. This is found in rule seven of lectionary rules in Common Worship (p 540), which is as follows:

During the period from the First Sunday of Advent to the Presentation of Christ in the Temple, during the period from Ash Wednesday to Trinity Sunday, and on All Saints' Day, the readings shall come from an authorized lectionary. During Ordinary Time (that is, between the Presentation and Ash Wednesday and between Trinity Sunday and Advent Sunday), authorized lectionary provision remains the norm but, after due consultation with the Parochial Church Council, the minister may, from time to time, depart from the lectionary provision for pastoral reasons or preaching or teaching purposes.

A closed season is when you are supposed to follow the lectionary. An open season is when you are free to depart from that provision, after consultation with the PCC.

This arrangement has been set in *New Patterns for Worship* diagrammatic form as follows:

### Services of Holy Communion

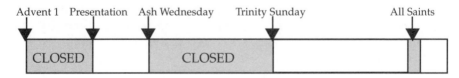

This gives the local church freedom to adapt the lectionary in the open season as well as using the lectionary readings themselves for a series in the closed seasons. Three examples should illustrate the possibilities.

## First Example: From Year B Open Season

Looking at Year B, the continuous reading for the principal service runs this way:

| Proper | OT | Epistle | Gospel |
|--------|-----|---------|--------|
| 4–7 | 1 Samuel | 2 Corinthians | Mark |
| 8–9 | 2 Samuel | 2 Corinthians | Mark |
| 10–11 | 2 Samuel | Ephesians | Mark |
| 12–14 | 2 Samuel | Ephesians | John |
| 15–16 | 1 Kings | Ephesians | John |
| 17 | Song of Songs | James | Mark |
| 18–20 | Proverbs | James | Mark |
| 21 | Esther | James | Mark |
| 22–25 | Job | Hebrews | Mark |

This suggests a number of possible series. The continuous readings cover many books sequentially. The importance is to get a balance. I chose to preach 3 series from these lessons:

| | |
|---|---|
| Propers 4–16 | Old Testament: Samuel, David and Solomon |
| Propers 17–21 | Mark |
| Propers 22–25 | Hebrews |

The idea was to get some sequential biblical teaching simply using the lectionary as a tool. I did not change the lessons, just chose to preach on one particular track. This covered a variety of services—Holy Communion, Evensong and family services. In the rota I indicated which reading I would preach from which sometimes meant an Old Testament lesson at 8 o'clock, where usually it was omitted. What I had done is to create a controlling lesson from the lectionary and preach from that. The balance of this might be questioned but the 13 weeks on Old Testament proved to be extremely popular both with myself as a preacher and with the congregation.

## Second Example: From Year A Open Season

A different church took an approach that slightly modified the lectionary, but this illustrates how easy this is with the present principal service lectionary. There is a four-week period in Year A where Philippians is the Epistle (proper 20 to proper 23). This begins 18–24 September, and then there are two weeks on 1 Thessalonians prior to Advent and a long period on Romans prior to this. They wanted to have a nine-week series to cover the autumn term. What they did therefore was to expand out in both directions the reading from Philippians to give this longer series while not changing any of the other readings:

| Proper | RCL Reading | Local Adaptation |
|--------|-------------|------------------|
| 17 | Romans 12.9–21 | Philippians 1.1–11 |
| 18 | Romans 13.8–14 | Philippians 1.12–30 |
| 19 | Romans 14.1–12 | Philippians 2.1–11 |
| 20 | Philippians 1.21–30 | Philippians 2.12–18 |
| 21 | Philippians 2.1–13 | Philippians 2.19–30 |
| 22 | Philippians 3.4b–14 | Philippians 3.1–11 |
| 23 | Philippians 4.1–9 | Philippians 3.12–4.1 |
| 24 | 1 Thessalonians 1.1–10 | Philippians 4.2–9 |
| 25 | 1 Thessalonians 2.1–8 | Philippians 4.10–23 |

What this has done is expanded the four weeks on Philippians to cover the whole book in a nine-week series rather than a four-week series that partially covers the book. The beauty of RCL is that with continuous readings this can be done without having to change the rest of the lectionary provision as the continuous reading means there is no theme each week. And the way that the Church of England has authorized the Revised Common Lectionary means that you are within the regulations of lectionary use if you choose to do this sort of thing. Thus one set of readings can be expanded to preach on a whole book.

## Third Example: Sundays of Easter Closed Season

The Sundays from the Second Sunday of Easter in Year C have Acts as the first reading, Revelation as the second reading and John as the Gospel. John is not sequential. While the readings do not cover a whole book they would provide a series giving some of the flavour of either Acts or Revelation.

|          | Acts        | Revelation      |
|----------|-------------|-----------------|
| Easter 2 | 5.7–32      | 1.4–8           |
| Easter 3 | 9.1–6       | 5.11–14         |
| Easter 4 | 9.36–43     | 7.9–17          |
| Easter 5 | 11.1–18     | 21.1–6          |
| Easter 6 | 16.9–15     | 21.10, 22–22:5  |
| Easter 7 | 16.16–34    | 22.12–14        |

In Years A and B the first reading is also extracts from Acts. But in Year A the Epistle is 1 Peter and in Year B 1 John. Again these are extracts but in six weeks they cover a substantial part of the book.

|          | Year A 1 Peter   | Year B 1 John |
|----------|------------------|---------------|
| Easter 2 | 1.3–9            | 1.1–2.2       |
| Easter 3 | 1.17–23          | 3.1–7         |
| Easter 4 | 2.19–25          | 3.16–24       |
| Easter 5 | 2.2–10           | 4.7–21        |
| Easter 6 | 3.13–22          | 5.1–6         |
| Easter 7 | 4.12–14; 5.6–11  | 5.9–13        |

This is another possibility of book-based sequential preaching.

## Some Consequences

These three simple approaches do have some consequences. Firstly you need to hold in mind a wider view of what is going on. From year to year you will need to monitor what you have done to get a balance between Gospel, Epistle and Old Testament. The more you diverge from the lectionary the more important this will become, otherwise you will be in danger of preaching on your favourite passages (I have a delight in Old Testament narrative). The selection of the series ought also to relate to the vision of the congregation or the mission action plan. If you are doing a series with selections from a book you will need to look at the integrity of the selection. The lectionary compilers have already done this for you. However, local factors may well overrule and this might suggest a lectionary change. Various local celebrations (for example church or team anniversary) might be incorporated into this, but sometimes these lead to a break in the series, a problem we noted Augustine having. Indeed you might need to plan the whole thing around these local factors. So there is a need to consider the whole lectionary package.

There are also consequences for the preachers. They will need to be disciplined and work together at least to agree to follow a common trajectory. It may be that they need to listen to God, the congregation, and one another to decide which passages to concentrate on. Some of the passages are easier than others. Hebrews proved to be quite difficult and I wondered if I was tackling more than I was capable of. In the end I was quite relieved to have only had a short go at it rather than preach the whole book. Likewise with David there were some quite difficult passages, but next time round I might be tempted to take the second approach and vary the readings more to get different sections of the story into the series.

# Modular Lectionary Material

4

## Why Do We Have This Material?

The New Patterns for Worship provides a wealth of off-the-peg modules for sermon series. *Patterns for Worship* has always included some modular lectionary material. It was included in the original report of 1989 and in the first edition in 1995. This built on the idea that in certain seasons there was lectionary freedom. The first two versions however only included four examples, all of which are included in the *New Patterns for Worship*. Some congregations had gone in for variation of the readings from the lectionary from time to time. What *Patterns for Worship* tried to do was to model good practice by keeping the readings fixed around the two key seasons of Christmas and Easter, while allowing variations in the rest of the year. While making some common practices legal, this also posed a question about what are the best readings for any local church. Freedom also brings choice and this might call into question whether always following the lectionary is the best option.

## Open and Closed Seasons in the Service of the Word

The lectionary provision discussed in the last chapter related to the Principal Service, particularly when it is a eucharist. Within the *Service of the Word* there are slightly different rules for open seasons and closed seasons. This is found in note 5 in the *Service of the Word* (*Common Worship* p 27), which says:

> **Readings**
> There should preferably be at least two readings from the Bible, but it is recognized that if occasion demands there may be only one reading. It may be dramatized, sung or read responsively. The readings are taken from an authorized lectionary during the period from the Third Sunday of Advent to the Baptism of Christ, and from Palm Sunday to Trinity Sunday. When *A Service of the Word* is combined with Holy Communion on Sundays and Principal Holy Days, the readings of the day are normally used.

This is summarized in the following chart:

*Services other than Communion*

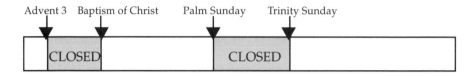

The dates are slightly different between a *Service of the Word* and the Communion lectionary. However, both allow a significant period when departing from the lectionary is permissible. Curiously this does not allow for variation in Lent at Communion. There has been a tradition in some circles of a Lenten series. This is in part because of the desire in the closed seasons to keep to a common lectionary. This might have been addressed by providing some Lenten modules as an option within the main lectionary provision. Perhaps this is to come.

In the open seasons variation is permitted for pastoral or preaching reasons. In a *Service of the Word* there may be only one reading, but there is encouragement to have at least two in order not to cut the amount of Scripture in worship. It may be necessary to compose a collect to fit the readings, a practice that is allowed by *Common Worship* (see p 22, last sentence).

## Sample Modules

*New Patterns for Worship* produces 46 sample modules. They cover much of the Old Testament and large parts of the new. The longest module is eight weeks and the shortest is three weeks long. They are constructed on some of the following principles:

- There is a brief title to the series (for the Old Testament modules).
- There is a controlling lection (printed in bold), which gives the preaching passage.
- A liturgical response is provided for possible use in the service.
- They are samples that you can adapt for local use or develop to compose your own.
- You may have to interrupt the series, for example for harvest.

This is a rich and varied provision. With some thought and preparation this might provide a number of years of material for preaching.

# What If I want To Compose My Own Material?

This question is given some guidance in note 6 (p 106). This says that when you design your own reading scheme you should ensure:

- That there is an adequate amount of Scripture;
- That justice is done to the balance of the book;
- That justice is done to the balance of Scripture;
- That appropriate gospel passages are included if there is Holy Communion;
- That the church council or appropriate lay group is involved in decisions.

This contains some important points:

- Some people use the *Service of the Word* to minimize the readings, often only having one. Is this sufficient exposure to Scripture?
- It is too easy to skew the meaning of a book by only looking at some areas and ignoring others, for example ignoring Jesus' eschatological material.
- Some people seem tempted to have one reading at say *A Service of the Word with Holy Communion* that is controlled by the preaching. Even if this is an Old Testament story, a gospel has to be included.
- Decisions for change are not just for the incumbent.

What this fails to talk about is the preaching team. This might include a number of people—incumbent, Reader, retired clergy, all may take their part preaching. A sermon series requires some co-operation between them to produce an agreed strategy and a review when it is completed.

In order to encourage preachers to take up this provision for their own sermon series I am now going to present three modules and give a commentary on their production. These are only my examples and you may feel that some of the choices are not the best. However, the aim of doing this is to encourage you to try, and to realize some of the issues in doing it. The process is quite complex and demands a good knowledge of the Scripture and its interpretation.

# First Worked Example

The following has been developed as an example of material *not* provided by *New Patterns for Worship*, in order to look at some of the issues. The scenario considered is of a church that asks for some teaching on marriage and divorce. This is an attempt to provide a modular lectionary in the same style as those in *New Patterns*.

## Marriage and Divorce

Blessed are those who are invited to the wedding supper of the Lamb!
**These are the true words of God.**
Rev 19.9

|   | OT lesson | Psalm | Epistle | Gospel |
|---|-----------|-------|---------|--------|
| 1 | Genesis 2.18–24 | 67 | 1 Cor 6.12–20 | Mark 10.1–9 |
| 2 | Deut 24.1–4 | 127 | 1 Cor 7.12–16 | Matthew 5.27–32 |
| 3 | Genesis 29.14–30 | 128 | Eph 5.21–33 | John 2.1–11 |
| 4 | Hosea 2.14–23 | 45 | Rev 19.6–9 | Matthew 25.1–13 |

This module does something different from those in *New Patterns*. It takes an ethical issue that effects all in society in one way or another and puts it into a lectionary module. This, in and of itself, is difficult in that the teaching of the Scripture on marriage and divorce is scattered in the Bible. In four weeks it is impossible to look at every passage and so the question of having a balanced selection became foremost in my mind. This has resulted in the idea of a 'controlling lection' having to be modified, in the sense that it is not easy to make any one type of reading, for example the Epistle, the controlling lection.

The context is also a big consideration. In any congregation many will have been married, some will be divorced (and remarried), some single (some not wanting to be), and some will be widowed (and maybe tragically). There are likely to be a whole set of approaches to the subject, from those who hold an absolutist position to those who cannot see why the church has had such a hard time deciding to remarry people. Not only will great sensitivity be required in the preaching but this also influence choices. This was particularly difficult for the responses: how was one group not to feel excluded or put down? In the end the best decision seemed to take the eschatological theme as it applies to everyone, whatever his or her personal experience.

While not being able to follow a controlling lection method, for the reasons noted, an alternative approach was to theme each week as follows:

| Week 1 | one flesh |
| --- | --- |
| Week 2 | divorce |
| Week 3 | love |
| Week 4 | eschatology |

There is no particular order for these four weeks and it might make sense to invert weeks two and three to put the positive before the negative. The first week begins with Gen 2, which seemed to be a good starting point, and the last week ends with Rev 19, a clear ending.

Trying to get a balance of passages proved difficult at times. What is the best passage with an eschatological dimension from the Old Testament? In the more positive week it is difficult to find an Old Testament passage that doesn't have complications. Jacob brings you to polygamy; the story of David and Michal is full of Saul's hate for David. Tobit was tempting but then has the problems of using the Apocrypha and there is the sub-plot of death by demon on your wedding night! I did turn to Common Worship Pastoral Rites but found that marriage lections are not really going in the same direction, often being there to exhort the couple rather than to give a fulsome teaching on marriage. The wedding day is more for exhortation than expository teaching.

Some passages were left out that others might think are important. For example, there is nothing from the Song of Songs. A passage from this book might be right for week three, but then there is a cultural question. I think I wanted week three to be about love as the basis for marriage. This is very romantic, a position strongly defended in our society, but it is not the approach of the rest of the world or the Bible. While you do see marriage for love, you also see marriage being arranged, and marriage for political alliance. Would the use of Song of Songs here reinforce our culture without giving a critique that other passages of Scripture might bring? Perhaps the proposed weekly theme is being driven too much in my choice by popular culture at this point. The patriarchal families had an amazing amount of disfunctionality but were God's chosen way of working. This challenges the idealization of family in our culture.

The psalms were put in last (and here the Pastoral rites were used for inspiration). They seem to be most difficult to fit into any scheme based on a theme save the broadest connection. But their inclusion is important as any month of teaching might well include the monthly 'All Age' Service and evensong. The latter sees psalms as integral and the former needs to learn to include material from the psalms in the service, perhaps on overheads, or in the notice sheet, or in the order of service.

## Second Worked Example

This second example began as a conversation with a minister whose church had done a similar series. I am not quite sure which biblical women were looked at in the other church but this seemed a fruitful idea which I adapted. There are modules for women of faith in *New Patterns*, but they are from particular books of the Bible rather than a mixture of Old and New Testaments.

### Women of Faith

A woman who fears the Lord:
**She is to be praised.**
Proverbs 31.30

|   | OT lesson | Psalm | Epistle | Gospel |
|---|---|---|---|---|
| 1 | **Genesis 21.1–7** | 119.1–8 | Galatians 4.21–31 | Luke 11.27–28 |
| 2 | **Judges 4.1–8** | 119.33–40 | Romans 16.3–16 | Luke 8.1–3 |
| 3 | 1 Sam 1.1–2, 10–18 | 119.57–64 | Galatians 4.1–7 | **Luke 1.26–38** |
| 4 | 2 Chron 34.19–24 | 119.73–80 | Acts 18.1–22 | **John 20.10–18** |

I quickly chose Sarah, Deborah, Mary, and Mary Magdalene. These are representatives of many others who could have been chosen. The aim was to give a more global picture compared with the modules in *New Patterns*. It possibly needs a longer series. As the aim was to look at these people, the method of a controlling lection was used (the reading in bold), which is the key reading to preach from and around which the whole of the rest of the lectionary is constructed.

Although the psalms were chosen last, the idea of using extracts of Psalm 119 is to use this great Psalm to talk about the life of devotion and faith. Much of it is about obedience to God and his ways, and the cry of the heart when the psalmist fails. This seemed well related to a series on a life of faith.

The rest of the readings were surprisingly hard to find. In one way there is too much material, in another way (from our perspective) there are difficulties in the stories. Gen 21 was chosen as one of the happier stories of Sarah. It is immediately followed by her expulsion of Hagar. Maybe I have been too easy on Sarah and should have had the longer reading. This then might have made more sense of the Epistle, one of the few discussions of Sarah in the New Testament. Luke 11 was chosen to contrast with what might have been inferred from Genesis 21, that is, that women of faith are there simply to have children. Again I am conscious that other cultures today would be more sympathetic with that idea. So my choices here have a strong element of cultural conditioning. But I am also aware that one of the pitfalls of such a series is to present a patriarchal view that would put off many of the listeners. Maybe one of the aims of the series is to show that this is not the only reading of the texts.

Deborah as one of the judges is a very strong person and the men are seen as rather weak in the story. I wanted the theme of 'strong in faith' to prevail so I have the women ministering to Jesus as the Gospel and Paul's greeting at the end of Romans, which includes many women in the story. This entails a transfer from a literal battle to the battle of faith, but this is a move the New Testament makes and so seems quite justified.

For Mary, typology takes over. There seem to be many strong connections between the story of Hannah and Mary—childbirth, songs of praise, visits to the temple, special children. They both stand at the beginning of a significant narrative about God at work. The Epistle suggests that this is about becoming God's children.

Mary Magdalene is involved in a ministry of the word in announcing the good news. Huldah also has such a ministry, but this time bringing a word of judgment. Priscilla, likewise, has such a ministry with her husband.

The subtext I have mentioned became more apparent in reflecting on the choice of readings and thinking about alternatives. It was clear that this was a process of finding a theme that linked the readings. So two techniques have been used here—'controlling lection' and 'theme.'

My own more conservative bias might be seen in this series if it were to be compared to Phyllis Tribble's *Texts of Terror*.[12] This wonderful book is an exposition of the Scriptures, a fine example of narrative criticism, and a feminist approach. I am aware of the problems of patriarchy even if I don't always escape them myself. In preaching, these views must be taken into consideration, as they are likely to influence many in the congregation. Such a series will challenge both preacher and people as together they are confronted by Scripture and their different understandings of it. The readings might, at times, seem to reinforce the patriarchal criticism (or might have done if I had not excluded passages like Hebrews 11 which concentrates on *men* of faith), but the aim has been to bring out the sub-plot of women of faith found in the Scripture. It is this layer that the sermon series aims to uncover.

# Third Worked Example

I wanted to try to preach on a theological theme. To be safe I thought I would go for something that I was confident about and so chose baptism. While there is a personal agenda here I find that in evening classes I do on baptism people benefit much from a more systematic look at the issue. For folk who don't come to such activities the sermon might be their only point of teaching.

## Baptism

All who have been baptized into Christ:
**They have been clothed with Christ.**
Gal 3: 27

|   | OT lesson | Psalm | Epistle | Gospel |
|---|-----------|-------|---------|--------|
| 1 | *Genesis 6.9–22* | 29 | 1 Peter 3.18–22 | *Mark 1.9–13* |
| 2 | *Exodus 14.21–31* | 66 | *Romans 6.1–14* | John 3.22–30 |
| 3 | Joshua 3.14–4.7 | 46 | *Acts 2.37–47* | Mark 10.35–40 |
| 4 | 2 Kings 5.1–14 | 106.1–15 | Titus 3.3–7 | *Matthew 28.16–20* |

The vast riches of material were somewhat perplexing at times. Perhaps the first choice in constructing this module was to approach the Old Testament from a typological angle. This is sometimes contested as an approach but my recent reading of patristic works on baptism encouraged me to be bold. So I chose the Old Testament passages first and then begin to fit the rest together. I then worked on the Gospel, wanting to begin with Jesus' baptism and the Great Commission. The rest became a process of filling in, following, for example, lines of typology in the Epistle in Week 1.

I did not choose a controlling lesson approach and am closer to a theme, but I am not quite there. It is almost as if there are stronger lessons and weaker lessons. I have chosen to put the stronger lessons in italics. They all say things about baptism in different ways, but in preaching I might concentrate more on the stronger lessons and use the others as illustrations. As there are six stronger lessons it might mean that a better strategy would be to produce a six-week module and have a controlling lesson. But I can see that there are many passages about baptism and the problem might repeat. I can also see that I would like to produce a module on baptism in Acts, as there is a whole series of key baptismal passages just in this book. That would then be more like the modules provided in *New Patterns*, following the course of a book. But this example was an attempt to do something more systematic along a theme. Another way might have been to theme a week, and that way deal with infant baptism in one week. However, I wanted to start with letting the scriptures speak and be able to preach a more positive message before going on to points of controversy.

The refrain was influenced by an Orthodox chant but I went back to an original scriptural verse. The psalms try to pick up bits of the Old Testament story or have a typological link in some way. Psalm 106 also gives warning to the people of God about falling from the covenant and so gives a dimension for preaching not addressed in a direct way in the New Testament.

If I was able, I would like to see this series preached in a number of places and so some of the discussion about how to do this best could then be ironed out. In reality the local preacher or team gets one shot at doing a module like this and then has to go on to something else. This is challenging, daunting, and humbling because there is no doubt that hindsight will produce some better combinations. What is needed is a wisdom in forming the module that is soaked in the Scripture and a life of prayer.

## Summary

This chapter has looked at the modular approach of *New Patterns for Worship*. There is a significant provision here of off-the-peg lectionary modules that may well encourage churches to try a sermon series. I have continued to develop the previous argument but given worked examples to encourage you to write your own modules. In offering three modules and commenting on the issues the process has produced I hope I have shown the complexities— but that it will also encourage you to try this for yourself.

# 5

## Ordering the Preaching

*Teams of preachers need to meet to consider the plan for preaching.*

Much of the literature on the Common Worship lectionary has exhorted people to understand the lectionary principles and plan the preaching. But how is this planning to be done? What are the key questions in doing this? At the end of chapter three I began to raise some key points. I will conclude by looking at some of the issues and ways that they might be developed.

### Preaching Teams

The development of ministry teams has led to the preaching often being done by a team of people. This requires some coordination between them. At the basic level there has to be agreement to follow the lectionary and preach on one or more of the passages for the day. However, if the potential of the lectionary is to be realized then more is needed than this.

Perhaps the preachers could meet as one of the ministry sub-teams at least twice a year to look at what is coming up and make some plans. A variety of strategies have been identified in this booklet. The most simple in ordinary time is to preach along one of the tracks of continuous reading. This requires a decision by the group. A key thing that such meetings can also do is to identify resources. A sermon series on a book of the Old Testament may be quite a challenge and a group may have more ideas than one person working on his or her own. The Grove Biblical Studies Bulletins available online have provided a set of commentary reviews that might suggest some of the better works that a group might want to have available between them.[13]

### Questions for Review and Planning

In reviewing a whole range of questions might be asked about the teaching:

- What have we been teaching?
- Is there a balance between the topical and the expository?

What is needed is to consider what has been delivered over the last year and to think about it its adequacy.

In *The Art of Prophesying*, Perkins suggested that there were a variety of people in the congregation:

- Those with no faith.
- Those whose faith needs to grow.
- Those who have slidden from the road.

There are clearly people in different stages of faith in the congregation. Has a balance occurred over the year so that the preaching is directed to help them? There is nothing worse than to hear only evangelistic preaching when the whole congregation is converted. It might be helpful to think of the congregation in terms of stages of faith development and try to discern what preaching is appropriate for each stage.

In terms of balance there are two poles:

- The great truths of the faith
- The needs of the congregation

The two, of course, go together but have we done this over the last year and what do we plan to do in the next?

Then there are questions about growth through preaching:

- Are we seeing new people become Christians through the preaching ministry?
- Do we see people built up to become ministers themselves?
- Are we promoting wisdom, knowledge and holiness?

These are not always easy to answer but do need to be addressed.

This may seem like a counsel of perfection and we know we are earthen vessels. However, there is a time to look at the preaching we have been doing, reflect on it, and look at the possibilities of the future. The introduction of *Common Worship* encourages us to do this and provides a possibility of great biblical preaching in our congregations.

# Notes

1   P Benson and J Roberts, Grove Pastoral booklet P 92 *Counting Sheep: Attendance Patterns and Pastoral Strategy.*

2   See *The Master Christian Library* (AGES Software, 1997, CD ROM).

3   *The Master Christian Library*, p 326.

4   See G Lawless, 'Augustine of Hippo' in WH Willimon and R Lischer, *Concise Encyclopedia of Preaching*, (Louisville: Westminster John Knox Press, 1990) p 20.

5   See H O Old, *The Reading and Preaching of the Scriptures in the Worship of the Christian Church, Vol.4, The Age of the Reformation* (Grand Rapids: Eerdmans, 2002) p 37.

6   *Reading and Preaching*, p 148.

7   W Perkins, *The Art of Prophesying* (Edinburgh: Banner of Truth, 1606, 1996) p 79.

8   *The Art of Prophesying*, p 326.

9   W Temple, *Readings in John's Gospel* (London: Macmillan, 1950).

10  J R W Stott, *I Believe in Preaching* (London: Hodder and Stoughton, 1982) pp 315–317.

11  For example J R W Stott, *Only One Way: the Message of Galatians* (Leicester: IVP, 1968, 1976).

12  P Tribble, *Texts of Terror* (Philadelphia: Fortress Press, 1984).

13  Past issues of *Biblical Studies Bulletin* can be found on the Grove web site http://www.grovebooks.co.uk/ by clicking on the link on the home page. New issues are sent free to subscribers to the Biblical series.